Other books by James Armstrong

Monument in a Summer Hat

Blue Lash

Nature, Culture and Two Friends Talking (with Kim Chapman)

Crossings, the Poets Laureate of Winona, Minnesota (with Emilio DeGrazia, Ken McCullough and Nicholle Ramsey)

Empire

Poems

James Armstrong

Shipwreckt Books Publishing Company
357 W. Wabasha St.
Winona, Minnesota 55987

Library of Congress Control Number: 2023930180

Copyright 2023 Jim Armstrong
Copyright 2023 Shipwreckt Books
ISBN: 979-8-9875338-0-2

This book is dedicated to my brother.

Contents

Advent

First Snow 3
Season's Greetings 4
Cold Front 5
Advent 6
Bond 7
In The Bleak Midwinter 8
Cocktail 9
Weary Blues 10
Laid On the Wind 11
To Washington Crossing the Delaware 12
Solstice 2020 13
Evening Flurries 14
Kentucky, December 1969 15
Boxing Day 16
Knife River 17
To A Gar in Winter 18
Ritual 19

Empire

Military Statue in Inverness 23
Fair Haired Lads Pass 24
Loch Ness 25
Slighe 26
The Fall of Foyers 27
Still Life 1658 28
Officer And Young Girl Laughing 29
Sputnik 30
Elements 31
Empire 33
Immigrants 35
The Union 37

Off The Gunflint 39
American Toad 40
Sad Thoreau 41
Election Diary 42
Two Sandhill Cranes in Late March 45

Plague Year

New Year 49
Leviathan 50
San Antonio River 51
Outbreak 53
Disaster Capitalism 54
Birding in the Pandemic 55
Comus 56
Minneapolis 1942 57
Sonnenizio Based on a Line from Terrance Hayes 58
The Party 59
Ghost House 60
Wild Surmise 61
September 11 62
200,000 63
October 2020 64
Halloween Before an Election 65
The Count 66
Abendlied 67
The Coal Smoke of Terre Haute 68
December 8 69
Three Contemporaries 70
God 72
January 73
Radical Chic 74
American Carnage 75
Cocytus 76
Cups 77
Compost Site 78

Helicopter Sonnets

1. Training Flight 81
2. Qualifying Jump 82
3. Surfari 83
4. Why We Are in Vietnam 84
5. The Remains 85
6. They'll Do It Every Time 86
7. Figures in a Landscape 87
8. Apocalypse Now 88
9. Redux 89

The Tower Variations

Fall Palette

Out Of Eden 115
Rapturous Decay 116
Michigan Sonnet 118
Contemplating A Phrase from Lewis Mumford 119
Simmer 120
The Anthropocene 121
Say Yes to Michigan 122
Normal School 123
Polonius 125
Landscape 126
Against The Gnostics 127
Requiem 128
Pulling Out 129
Fall Palette 131

Notes 133

Acknowledgements 135

About the Poet 137

"When are men dangerous?"
—William Stafford

Advent

First Snow

As you lie in bed,
you can tell it has snowed
by the radiance in the window.
Light comes from the ground and not the sky
as if you suddenly lived on the moon.
In that moment, you are back to childhood
when any change of the exterior world
is a change of heart, when the light
tells you what to feel, when
you need the sky
and its endless changes.
As that first snow fell,
each snowflake whispered
a secret so intimate
it took the rest of your life to un-believe.
Here it is again.
Your chance to repent.

Season's Greetings

The congressman tweets
a photo of his family;
each child holds a machine gun.
His youngest cradles an Uzi.
His wife smiles uneasily.
Their Christmas tree
stares with all its lights.

I remember an autumn woods,
the cold stock of a Mauser
against my cheek.
The barrel was my eye, the
bullet my wish—it slept
in the magazine
under the bolt. With
a small quiver, my finger
caused the sun to leap
and a hole opened its mouth
in the target's center
across the ravine.
It was a distant event, but
I saw those mouths
could open anywhere.

Cold Front

What had been streams in the alley
hardens to brutal glass.
Clouds roar overhead,
blue-veined continents.

Powerlines and tree limbs
lie in the affronted road.
The house flinches
under the sky's cold fist.

We pity anyone who must go out
and wonder how animals
fare in that combing wind.
A rabbit crouches under a bush.

A crow on top of a cottonwood
surfs the clicking branches and,
with obsidian insolence,
shakes his wings at God.

Advent

I like those old-fashioned advent calendars,
rural scenes with glitter and die-cut windows
that open to change the picture with hidden images—
a lamb, a child's top, a little bird—things
we discover as if we hadn't put them there
in the first place. We know that we
made these pictures; we cut the holes. We know
in the real outdoors, there are hidden doors
and doors within those doors: an infinite
slamming and creaking of organisms, chemical
processes, centuries piled upon centuries,
causal chains, snakes swallowing their tails.
But I like this picture: snow, a barn.
A miraculous child who has just been born.

Bond

In the '80s I bought a shotgun,
used, from the Gun Barn on Highway 40.
It leaned up against the wall in my apartment
in an orange zippered case. Was it my wingman
in some twisted sense? I was the only guy
in my step-aerobics class. I liked working out
with middle-aged women. Was this a problem?
I caught flak for it at work. I went hunting
by the power plant, but never shot a duck.
When I was ten, all I wanted for Christmas
was a James Bond attaché case
that came with a pistol,
shoulder stock, silencer, scope—
all in plastic, of course. My mother wouldn't
buy it, she said. Not for Jesus' birthday.
She wouldn't give me a license to kill.

In The Bleak Midwinter

Chivington, having massacred Black Kettle's band
at Sand Creek, saw into the Republican heart:
darkness unrelieved by Calvary. The nails
had to be spared to build the Denver courthouse
with its Beaux-Arts gilding and oak trim.
In Georgia, the freed slaves would be slaves again;
someone had to pick cotton.
Black Kettle and White Antelope might stand
under the flapping of the American flag,
but this would not protect them—their death
must moisten the edges of money
and piety. Jesus, naked at Wounded Knee,
would have to be chipped out of the frozen ground
with an axe, so we could bury him again.

Cocktail

Out of all my thousands of childhood hours
in Terre Haute, why do I mostly remember
the yew hedge in front of the Hi-Life Lounge
I passed on the way to choir practice every Thursday?
The skies were always grey. I walked with Larry,
an older boy from the neighborhood.
We crossed Wabash Avenue, went past the
   shopping center
to the church, where we stood in the choir loft
and sang—was it "Be Thou My Vision"?
What part did I sing? Tenor? All I remember
is that dirty hedge in a brick planter, beneath which
a cocktail glass had fallen upright on the gravel.
Because I was small, I could always see it.
Sometimes it was full of snow, sometimes rain.

Weary Blues

Cousins, I'm tired of falling in love with tyrants.
I'm tired of Grandma opening the door for the wolf
because "I like him, he says what he thinks."
Later we see him wearing her Packers sweatshirt.
Snow, like shame, falls on everyone.
It deadens the postman's footsteps.
The television barks and barks.
The fist rejects the feathers of a caress,
hoards its small ration of darkness.
When we were small, we lived in a small world.
When we grew up, the sky went on forever
and we kept buying bigger hats.
Cousins, I'm tired of dreaming of a better past.
I'm tired of us standing in the snow
bareheaded, imagining a caress.

Laid On the Wind

for Robert Bly

A boy carries an automatic rifle
into town and shoots three people.
He is cheered on by old men
who have decided, why not
make a television show out of hatred?
There's money in it.
We came here a long time ago
on wooden ships.
We longed for a clearing
without privilege.
On the wall in my basement,
I've hung the rusting pieces
of an iron musket
my great-great grandfather shouldered
when he walked into the wilderness.
His trust was in the Bible, but
his God was in the powder horn.
"Jim," you ask, "why is
the musket in pieces?"

Jesus said:
The world will eat a gun
if you leave it out in the rain.

To Washington Crossing the Delaware

Dear General,
"Never stand up in a boat" is good advice
I learned at scout camp. Especially true
in December, in the dark, in a river
knocking with ice. History paints
with a mythic eye. Your priapic sword
and flapping cape, your Napoleonic waistcoat, your
destiny-fastened gaze—Leutze imagined these
on the far-away Rhine. German art students
stood in for patriots, shivering, hatless,
some without gloves or shoes, some
armed with fowling pieces and frontier muskets,
eager to assert their independence
by obeying a leader. Leutze added moon-gleam
to your military pigtail. Dear General,
you did a good deed by not becoming our emperor.
We won't mention your China teacups,
your slaves.

Solstice 2020

It is the longest night of the year. Just after supper,
the little boys next door stand in their front yard
and shout into the empty street. All year
they've gone without friends or school or grandparents
except in the small theater of their parents' laptop
and now they are yelling like maniacs—
one rings a bell, and the other bangs a pan with a spoon.
Above them, a half moon rides through clouds
that blow like the smoke of battle.
Goodbye, bad year. Run away from our shouts.
This night is as dark as it is going to get.

Evening Flurries

No sign of snow yet, just one white dove
over the rooftops. She would have loved
these rooftops—limestone caps above
Flemish brick. At the gable end, a little alcove
where you could set a saint or an apostle. She drove
all the way from Delft, but the stove
wouldn't light, so we went out to a sort of
late-night Chinese restaurant, where she called my bluff
over the Formica tabletop, her faux-fox cuff
trailing in the hoisin sauce. After she moved her stuff
out of the house, I got this apartment above
the Volvo dealership, but I kept one velvet glove
from the box she left behind—a kind of trove—
and her blue jean jacket that smells of Asian clove
cigarettes, and an old bandanna, wrapped around this
small framed print she loved:
a blue sky, a little poplar grove,
the pale blur of an out-of-focus dove.

Kentucky, December 1969

Early evening, snow crust on the back forty,
the air was damp but edged with cold
and smelled of fresh manure. The square bales
broke into flakes we kicked off the tailgate
as the Chevy moved slowly over the field
like a boat in a swell. The cattle came, lowing,
almost at a run, their pendulous shapes
dark against the snow, their winter coats
scruffy, their hooves loud on the hard
turf; breathing clouds of steam, drool
hanging from whiskered mouths, they
stopped, bowed to the dim stars of
hay that must have brought them
the hot mow of August, and the absent sun.

Boxing Day

The problem with Christmas is the day
after, empty bottles on the porch,
the tree still standing there
like an awkward boy after the dance,
the one who doesn't get
that you've moved on. The shepherds
suddenly remember their day jobs.
The star has set. Joseph
feeds cardboard into the brazier.
The child frets. Mary wraps her halo
in newspaper and packs it in a crate
with the candlesticks. The dove
in the top of the barn has flown.
The drooling ox nudges the manger.
In the distance, down by the river,
the waterwheel keeps on turning
as it did last night, and the night before.

Knife River

The cartouche of a snowshoe track
affixes my seal to the frozen river's
official document, already signed in the dash
and sniff of midnight by a doe's diacritics
punched in snowdrifts; by furtive grapeshot
beside up-flipped moss; by the faint
sutures of mice who've risked the open; by
the efficient rivet-holes of a fox
who went around the bend
on patrol. We all leave our dent
on the tapestry of nothing, below which
the river murmurs and chortles, or makes
a sound of wood blocks being tapped,
or, if you look down through
occasionally open hatches, shows
its black tongue between teeth of glass.

To A Gar in Winter

The backwater is lidded; the river narrows,
black and sluggish as the blood
of a hibernating animal. Deep under,
you drift in a starless channel,
a syringe in chainmail.
You hang under cathedral ceilings
where evening glows an arctic green.
O predatory missal, in which we read
everything holy and damned
and quick and finned, life goes, stays,
darts and bites, but sleeps also
in eddies of tugging chill. O gar,
rest your terrible jaws.
Let a poet transmit your dream.

Ritual

It's Three Kings Day, the official end
of Christmas. I set the gingerbread house
in the backyard, in moonlit snow, for the animals
wherever they are. Tonight will be twenty below.
Who knows what accommodation they seek?
Birds don't keep calendars. They're secular,
all fluffed out inside a bush. When I light
the votive candle, it flutters, catches—the
little sugar windows gleam. A model
of isolation has the charm real
wilderness can't keep. No kingly visitors
struggle across the drifting snow tonight
to pay homage with lavish gifts.
The moon is a half-spent coin.
The stars glitter. Tremble,
warm heart. You are at home.

Empire

Military Statue in Inverness

A Queen's Own Highlander in a pleated skirt
and ostrich feathers grasps his service carbine
like a drover's stick and stares across the Victorian
high street in front of the ScotRail station.

Couched at his stockinged knee, an unlikely
miniature Sphinx surveys the neatly
chiseled names of those on expedition
to Khartoum, Cairo, the battle of Tel-El Kabir.

Half of them died from fever and dysentery.
Down the street, the Highland Formal Wear
rent shop offers sporrans, Prince Charlie cutaways,

sgian dubhs, thistle cufflinks, the complete
drag show of imperial ethnicity.
The square reeks of sausage rolls and burnt coffee.

Fair Haired Lads Pass

The highland forest was a sodden sponge;
the path squelched beneath us as we clung
to the stoss and corkscrewed up the plunge
of Precambrian grindstones covered in moss

and swarming with midges. The view cleared off
to well-spaced birches and the barren loft
of knee-grazing heath—woody, tough
shrubs that kept their heads down and had just enough

ingenious flies to court them. Perhaps they thought
the dreich invigorating, for what
they could distill of it—
all that upland vacancy, drear and hushed.

Perhaps no one else wanted it?
Someone had though, once, fair-haired or not.
Someone had been pushed off, leaving us
the Loch's blue look, and plenty of desolation.

Loch Ness

Twenty-six miles of glacial trench
shivered with peatish water; the torn gusts
drove squadrons of foam across the reach
barren as it was deep. The relict forest

clung to the glen's drop like a green kilt.
The villages were stony, somnolent;
Urquhart Castle, a dynamited remnant.
Such basalt abandonments

demand, like any void, a compensation
which the brochures hasten to depict:
a phantom, offered to the camera's click
or appearing as a sonar blip,

a smudged dragon, corporeally aloof,
equally derided as a slick
of motor oil, a sea bird, or a joke—
the infinite regress, the veiled face of proof.

Slighe

It's a steep path down to Invermoriston
from the high road, all switchbacks and stone bridges;
almost as hard as the way up, where at treeline
we stand among bracken and midges

to peer beneath the scuffed face of the loch
for a crannog the guidebook said had been found by a
   monk
in a diving helmet. No luck. Lichenous rocks
at the top shelter trees, heather clings to the chinks,

scabrous and brave. We eat lunch in a drystone clochán
in wind-roar, then plunge down the ridge
through alleys of fir and pine, hypothermic and sodden,
through the town and its angry rapids and Georgian bridge

to St. Columba's well, by the roar of lorries.
A dark eye, a shrunken pool of stories.

The Fall of Foyers

Bright northern morning. The sun slants through trees
and the spray rises up from the linne.
Red squirrels chatter on the path. Five percent
of their ancient forest remains. The lees

stoke interest—signs, maps, interventions. Scotland
wants its own back. British Aluminum
stole the burn's flow, ran it through hydroelectric turbines
for a smelter on the loch. The Luftwaffe bombed them

in '41. War defined a homeland. From the parapet
we stare down the sheer face where the torrent pours
in an eldritch racket: the white roar
of becoming. On the bank, bluebells and violets

dewed by mist. Where is home, then?
Home is in motion.

Still Life 1658

Jan Janzs van de Velde (1620-1662)

Where are you? In darkness,
at the edge of a table. What
kind of tavern has no windows
or customers? You can see only objects
you'd find if you lit a match
in a cave that was also a crime scene. Bereft
of context, you keep trying to read the clues
to detect who ended the party. The jug seems
the main culprit, the raised cartouche
glitters on its swollen midriff like a terrible scar
rimmed with brown stains. The crackled glaze
echoes the cheap pearlescent glamour
of the shucked oyster shell. Everything's lurid
at this late hour, even the fruit. The jug's
unstoppered. The cards are played. The wine
dimly trembles. The lemon is damply nervous.
You've gone past merrymaking
and drunken singing to find the bleary grief
that made you drink in the first place. The pipe
is broken; the rope molders away. A voice says,
"You'll be moderately successful. You'll die
in your forties. Your widow will outlive you
by 30 years. The harbor will fill with silt."

Officer And Young Girl Laughing

Johannes Vermeer, c. 1657

The black sombrero, the scarlet officer's coat
with its pewter buttons, the linen shirt
that balloons from the cuff: these flag his income.
With his left hand he strokes
his heroic chin. Might he be mistaken? Is this
an opportunity for negotiation?
Her smile, her satin bodice, the glass of wine
that trembles in northern light, her small hand
lying so near, so enticingly open . . .
perhaps she is only making a friendly gesture,
as in, "I grant you that point, friend."
Her laughter makes him nervous.
Above them, afternoon shadows darken.
The casement, with its leaded panes, swings open.
The breeze smells faintly of salt
and fish. On the wall, a recent map
of West Friesland's harbor
bristles with ships.

Sputnik

I was born the month the Russian moon
crossed the night sky beeping
like a frenetic alarm,
America still yawning
at the factory gate
having just saved democracy
for Walt Disney and General Motors—
maybe in that order.
You could smell the aluminum
of a thousand tracts where women
high on hairspray and *Good Housekeeping*.
sent their children off
to a world terrified
by its victories.
The future seemed buzzy as neon
outside the Tastee-Freeze,
bright as the yellow coat of arms
of the fallout shelter
tacked to the courthouse entrance.
We'd grow up in fear
and polyester, television
our forever. In Sunday
school we watched
a movie about the Holocaust
and shivered to think that
someplace else
people could be so mean.

Elements

1.
When you left for Sweden, I went every day
to the path you had shown me,
a place from your childhood.
There was a small pool, shaded with low trees,
and if I looked into it,
I could sometimes see the still
form of a minnow
hanging in the light.
It was somehow you—
buoyant, breathing slowly,
taking the world inside yourself
with a clear gaze and delicate fins.
I wanted to shout,
"Why do you live down there
in a different element?"
The wind marred the pool's surface.
You disappeared.
And that was the beginning of
my apprenticeship.

2.
I wandered far those years.
Rode a bicycle through Scotland
and saw your face in a vault boss of Melrose
Abbey—that ruined place
where a people had changed their mind
and left their god
propped up under a shattered nave.

The river was beautiful.
The hills were beautiful.
The rain was just old trembling
made charming by distance.
I stood for a long time under the fallen roof,
doing my imitation
of the 19th century,
sketching you in pencil,
your dreaming medieval face
at the apex.
The waves of your stone hair.
Someone—a stone cutter—had seen you,
and said "Angel,"
and put you beyond the rain's tears.

Empire

I slept on the deck
of the overnight ferry to Tunis.
Salt rime of night,
tremor of engines,
wet vowels of the sea.
I say sleep: it was
more an extended reverie,
the radar turning and turning
like the head of an owl,
waves thudding the ferry's steel.
It was August 1979,
so many young people like me
on holiday from their lives,
their hair wind-tousled
as they huddled with backpacks and sweaters
and bottles of wine. Others
sat slightly apart,
dark-eyed men
with three-day stubble.
Their wives carried plastic bags
full of bread and olives
and shushed their children
who were fussing, rubbing their eyes.
We were all heading south
on the flow of money and time,
late in the American century,
heading toward the city
Aeneas abandoned long ago.
City of souks,

of pungent stalls,
city of ruined Roman baths,
city of hushed suburbs
guarded by machine guns,
city where men in robes
sat in cafes
and drank foamy coffee
from tall glass beakers
and watched young women
clicking across the ancient stones
in French heels
and Jackie O sunglasses.
City whose queen once,
consumed by grief and rage,
went up in a beacon of flame.

Immigrants

We shipped out of Londonderry
with only the clothes
on our backs.
Our wooden shoes
clacked on the deck.
In the foul air
below, the tin cup
we shared was chained to a post.
The waves pitched up
tall as Cave Hill over Belfast—
the wind nearly took our language.
Ten weeks on hardtack,
then we docked.
They made us wait.
If we were sick
we'd die on board, not
in their new world.
We didn't die,
we disembarked
and walked past Penn's tree
and left the wharf
for the muddy streets.
Ahead of us were the mountains.
We bought guns and chickens
and the ox. And the axe.
We already carried
our Ulster songs
about adultery and loss,
missing a place you've

been kicked out of,
killing the one you love.
We had our talent
for vengeance
and God.

And we brought the smallpox.

The Union

Along the
low shore
at Two Harbors
the high waves bit
and hard rain
drained until red mud
coated the beach stones.
A line of birches
leaned precariously;
now and then one
fell with a green crash
and lay in the surf
head-first, but
if you looked
under the torn bank
you saw intestinal cables,
thick and prehensile,
sprouting new saplings,
cantilevered
over the void. Who knew
that underground
serpent life? Who thought
that every old birch, rough
and lichen-fissured,
and every pale sapling
raising its insignia
against the dawn, all

clasped each other,
in the ochre underground, all
locked muscular legs together,
braced each other
against the iron waves?

Off The Gunflint

A trail of snapped things,
thickets nipped
thoughtfully.
A cold sashay.
Someone wore soup pots
as snowshoes
and postholed
the blue snow,
each print its own
thought. Anyone
that big did not need
to hurry. Where
are you, yellow incisors,
petroleum gaze,
octopus lips? Horsehair
couch with
chorus-girl knees,
rack of spreading cartilage?
Gone, leaving only these
cold wells of hunger
across the nothing of winter.

American Toad

Anaxyrus americanus

On the trail at Split Rock it crouches
under a heart-shaped leaf—
a shelf fungus with an instinct
for up, but no wings. Its leap
hurdled it over the ostrich ferns
to land audibly in leaf litter where
it gathered itself again,
pale skin stretched over trembling organs,
a dry little pudding with a
predatory watchfulness,
toothless mouth and adhesive tongue
ready to snap at occasions.

Sad Thoreau

It's November. All the leaves are down
and skittering, the ducks have flown
and the moon waxes high above the streetlights.
Was Thoreau sad because he had to leave
this life? A Christian holds the world on lease,
thinking to trade up when the market's right.
A Stoic has no exit out of this.
I have my own illusions. So do you.
Are we headed somewhere, a ghostly father
to chalk the path? If the world is not a copy
the dark falls deeper,
love grows sharper. The price of things gets dearer.
Thoreau was sad, and his pond grew nearer.

Election Diary

November 8, 2016

4 a.m.: a freight train
rattles the necklaces on
my wife's bureau.
I lie in bed, dreaming
of Tom Waits, who says,
"We've torn up the earth
like an old Christmas card."

4:45 a.m.: on the news,
a frac-caused earthquake
shakes Oklahoma. Eighty buildings
damaged, but "The refinery
is untouched."

6:30 a.m.: at the fire station,
rubber boots in a line, coats hanging
by the gleaming trucks.
Smell of oil and newly-painted concrete.
White-haired women at folding tables
with printouts, everyone polite
and feeling important. The ballot
they hand me feels
flimsy, like a high-school test,
little bubbles to darken. Stressed,
I read it twice.
Three times. It's hard to focus
and stay in the lines.

3:30 p.m.: down Highway 61
in the late afternoon,
in the distant folds of the bluff,
shadows grow
great violet rivers. The earth
turns its back on the sun, and
I am invisible from space,
as are the billions of cells
that I am made of—all of them
holding hands as the night comes on.
In the rooms of the forest, yellow leaves
glow like candles. Spectral light,
the gold of sacrifice.

7:30 p.m.: watching the returns
I notice
my "I Voted" sticker
is curiously similar
to the one they gave me
when I donated blood.

November 9, 2016

8:00 a.m.: No sleep since they called it
at four. I lie in bed
shivering as if with the flu. Finally
drift into vague semi-consciousness.
Might as well get up,
grind the coffee
and pour the milk. Let inertia
sweep me into the day.
Shower and shave and go to work.
The building is empty, all lit up
like the Titanic.

November 13, 2016

7:00 p.m.: in the brand-new high school auditorium
in Kasson, Minnesota. It's the school musical:
children in pajamas are onstage singing
"These are a few of my favorite things."
The backdrop of Austria trembles.
A boy with a Nazi armband appears,
his face the stone mask of hatred.
In the orchestra pit, the woodwinds cringe.
Outside the building, the wind howls in the parking lot.
One of William Stafford's little prairie towns,
an island of streetlights amid dark fields:
one of those places where anything can happen.

Two Sandhill Cranes in Late March

On the muddy
fisherman's path
to the swollen river
that spills its
cold silver
over the bank and
breeches the
ochre palisade,
two abrupt
silhouettes
rise from the grass,
incline their
Martian foreheads,
spread their
black capes,
open their
sharp beaks,
utter cries
awkward and terrible—
the wrenching
of clapboards
from some
long-abandoned
church,
the shriek
of nails
pulled from the
joists
of the world.

Plague Year

New Year

Front page of the hotel newspaper this morning:
smoke from the embassy compound
in Baghdad. The flutter of Hezbollah flags.
Last night in Times Square, Steve Harvey recited gags
for a crowd of one million. When they laughed, the sound
must have been like ten oceans. Dawn
over Minneapolis: tall buildings smoke
in 20-degree air, the sidewalks are slick with snow,
a few people walk quickly to work
in first light. Money doesn't take a day off.

Last night, when we came through the lobby,
revelers stood waiting for their ride. A woman
in a party dress swiped the screen on her phone.
It was 11:15. She still had so many options.

Leviathan

Autocrats love the people's love, not the people
crying out in anger, pain, or shame.
Quiz history—you will find the same
unanimous verdict. The boss is gleeful
if you are shouting his name. If not the
Tin Pan Alley of praise, then the Beale Street of outrage,
taken as testimony to his sexual wattage.
Ever in the night of the narcissist, we haven't got
disinterested candles. The only sin is indifference.
Now the Republic kneels, half dizzy, half drunk,
each faction feels the cleaving funk
vivisecting the union—vertiginous deference
edge-walks the headlong descent,
revolving in the vacuum inside the tyrant.

San Antonio River

"We must labour to be beautiful."
    —*W.B. Yeats*

1.
Texas, early spring. The River Walk
at 7 a.m. Bald cypresses and oaks
unfurl their delicate green. The river's pace
is languid. Two men steer a workboat

cautiously upstream, bringing plastic flats
of greenhouse annuals they'll use to replace
those that failed to keep their loveliness
intact. The men bring shovels, compost, tarps,

yellow work gloves. The grumble of their engine
disturbs the morning. When their wake
arrives, it slaps the levee. Reflections undulate

and fracture. Then the mirror grows still again.
Above, in a cypress, a heron brings to its mate
a stick. She tucks it carefully into place.

2.
Matthew 8:20

On a bench by the river, with a sleeping bag
pulled over his head, only his torn Jordans
stick out into the morning. The river's slack
glamour trembles in the wind.

Because the police haven't made their rounds,
the man is deep in his dream beside a bridge
underlit with bright reflections. But privilege
will clear away whoever troubles us. Two doors down

in front of the Hard Rock Café, a waiter
unchains the patio chairs and drags them out
with a metallic screech. A workman turns a spigot
and sluices off the piss-smell of the night.

What underwrites our peace? In equal parts:
ruthlessness, and calibrated innocence.

Outbreak

From the outset it was a ghostly threat
visible only to the forensic imagination,
untouchable, a rumor, a sudden stirring of wind
on the far side of a pond—seen, not felt,

but heard, as I did in the Arkansas truck stop
next to the men's room, by cans of Monster drink
and bags of Old Dutch pretzels: "Do you think,"
asked the man in a hoodie and Red Wing high tops,

"If I've been scrubbing my hands in the faucet
for two minutes straight, that'll kill it?"
He'd heard there were cases in Springfield.
On that drive up from Houston, the numbers followed me

like blackbirds—schools shut down, shops closed,
flights cancelled. The radio was full of anxious voices,
a sudden seriousness, a collective intake of breath.
Narrowing choices. The slowing of the world.

Disaster Capitalism

That was the month that Andrew Jackson's teeth
grew sharper, and every bill began to bite
the hand that fed it. We all felt it. Every week,
numbers grew terrible; by the whites

of their eyes we recognized the victims
who were suddenly essential. Nurses, cleaners, cooks,
meatpackers, bus drivers. Mail carriers. While the sleek
aesthetics of our new devices

fed on the glossy bonfires of the planet,
children went hungry. Who would make us great again?
"Us" meaning those ruthless enough to profit from it,
the hilarious pogrom. The original sin

was not apple picking, honey.
It was money.

Birding in the Pandemic

Dawn breeze scuffs the lake.
A hunting pack of pied-billed grebes
appears and disappears in the grey chop.
Last night: too much whiskey, too much news.
I have a hangover—or is it a fever?
I side-eye the jogger who coughs
coming up the path.
The chickadee—voluble, cheery fluff
in the top branches of an ornamental plum—
calls for normal relations. Was it naïve
to know the world has always been
a dark thicket, and not to think
I would be made to feel it?
It's hard to feel it, at the top.

Comus

Swedish whisky is as good as Scottish whisky
is as good as Duluth whiskey, depending on
the bottle and the circumstance. Dawn
may come on the hurt head as briskly
as it does at 6 a.m.—daylight, birdsong,
wind—the cost of your enchantment
diminishes what your bacchanal meant
last night. Elation is effervescent. Before long
what's remembered is the access to regret
that surfaced with your excess—a jet
of unexpected strength—and yet,
with aspirin and coffee, you might still forget
the blurry tears in all things,
the radiation that the heart emits.

Minneapolis 1942

from an old advertisement

Sleizer's 21 Club on South 8th:
chrome-legged bar stools, china lamps, padded booths,
wallpaper that matches the livid green skirt
of the hostess in a sailor hat who flirts
when you say you'll be shipping out in a special Pullman.
The war is on. The streets are full of uniforms
and the sudden fellow-feeling of . . . promise? Doom?
Tonight you'll supper in the Chandelier Room
For $1.75. You must see and hear Johnny O'Leary
the satirical Irishman—he plays two shows nightly.
Will you have the chow mein or the chicken?
Rollie Anderson on his Hammond Organ
is playing Glenn Miller's "American Patrol."
Your choice of potatoes. Butter and a roll.

Sonnenizio Based on a Line from Terrance Hayes

for George Floyd

    History is beyond me. I will need a black suit and umbrella
        now.
    History is what we read when the ashes cool.
    The world does not suit us, it is too cruel,
    but you and I need to live in it somehow.
    The world is beyond me, it's a force that presses down
    like an iron presses a suit, presses along
    the crease, which is a wrinkle I will allow,
    as opposed to those I need to flatten out.
    An umbrella, when it opens, flattens out
    its complications—which are unfolding now.
    Who is in charge? Who will need soothing?
    What do we need that we are burning now?
    Did it suit us to put a man in the ground?
    History is beyond me. I will need a black suit and umbrella
        now.

The Party

Is her whiteness more white because she was the color of pale honey?
    —Jack Gilbert

The back of my hand, forested with hairs
of blond and brown and darker brown. The
bamboo plait of wrinkles where the wrist must turn,
the tunnels of tendons that stretch
like hawsers from the knucklebones—
sand hills under which the blue veins shine.
So many shades—caramel and beige, parchment,
shell-pink of the nail beds. Rose of my palms.
Never anything you would nominate
as white. That plaster no-tint
was always a lie, like Las Vegas or heaven—
trying to throw a party where there is none.
Party of walls. Mardi Gras of flags and guns
diverting the common blood that runs and runs.

Ghost House

Once there was a house haunted by a ghost
who stayed put. The house was mortar and brick;
the ghost was tenebrous, of bespoke spirit-cloth,
gauzy and ungrasped. The people gasped
when the ghost fluttered. But nothing changed,
although the house often changed
sides, was gussied, gaudied, refurbished, burned
down once and rebuilt. Still, the ghost would abide.
Holidays came, and wars were fought and won;
the ghost sat on the porch and rocked and rocked.
Inside the house, on the famous desk, papers were signed.
Peace was declared. The ghost sighed in the pen.
Everyone said: "I wish that ghost were gone."

The ghost stayed on.

Wild Surmise

There's no place to go. There's the ocean to stop you.
   —John Steinbeck

America, you huff liberty like a kid huffs glue.
You have nothing else: no cooking, no delicate
graves, no old walls softened by flowers
to remind you of the limits of politics.
Your mountains were named for people you killed
as you were passing through on horseback.
You camped by a river, claimed it for God, and rode on.
America, you have nothing to distract you
from your disappointment that those golden towns
were only a rumor, light on a far canyon.
The fountain of your childhood is a dry cistern.
What was the lesson Balboa learned
when the Pacific startled him?
America, you have to live here or nowhere.

September 11

The radio announcer says a man
whose son died in the tower flames
has died of COVID-19.
Of the son, it was said he feared heights and fire.
Of the father, his greatest fear was the death of his son.
So, in that sense, he had lived fearlessly
for 19 years. Is grief
just fear in retrospect?
Both father and son died gasping for breath.
Both were killed by causes indifferent to them,
betrayed by men in power who did not keep watch.

200,000

September 23, 2020

I was eating cereal with milk
I was reading the L.L. Bean catalog
I was dusting the top of the door frame with a cloth
I was buttoning up my blue shirt
I was sitting in the bathroom reading a sonnet
I was in my office, deleting emails, opening new ones
I was practicing "Hello Stranger" on my guitar
I was gazing out the window at a goldfinch
I was picking up the newspaper from the sidewalk
I was looking at a picture of the president
I was looking at the peculiar mouth of the president
I was looking at the darkness inside that mouth

October 2020

Yesterday, my birthday; sudden snow,
fine-grained and wet, blurred the leaves
of the Norway maple and slicked the sidewalk,
a mixed message in a difficult season.
Should I linger? Press right on into the dark?
This was the fall we heard whitethroats tuning up
before sunrise in the reeds by Highway 61.
Flutes-only orchestra. Silent road.
This was the fall we saw the beaver slowly
swimming west, just offshore,
etching the lake in a widening V.
This was the fall we saw a wolf cross the median.
This was the fall we nervously counted yard signs
and face masks lying among the fallen leaves.

Halloween Before an Election

The moon, poetic warhorse, hangs in the sky
like the frontispiece of *Evangeline*.
The lake reflects it as a lustrous tongue
of riffled pearl. It's 6 a.m.
Orion is doing a handstand on the bluff;
I recognize him by the glitter of his belt.
Samhain was thin time for Celts—
ghosts crossed over to harangue their relatives.
Across 61, the graveyard is as quiet as a ghost.
Celts were head-hunters; their jack-o'-lanterns
were grisly trophies. In the rising wind
by the lake the cottonwood hisses through broken teeth.
Yard signs shudder in the moonlight.
The headless horseman of the Republic rides.

The Count

November 8, 2020

An eagle in a tree halfway up the bluff—
at this distance, a grain of rice.
But once I've seen it, I can find it again.
Last night, speeches out of Wilmington,
fireworks; a flight of drones
spelled out the politician's name
against the Atlantic darkness.
This morning is weirdly calm;
the sun casts long shadows
across orange hills. The still lake
trembles at the cartwheel
of a leaf. All I can think of
is a friend who sat, once,
in a predawn Michigan wood,
shotgun across his lap.
Light filled the spaces
between bare treetops,
a chickadee tried out a call.
My friend reached
to scratch his neck,
and the morning exploded—
throwing splinters and bark
two inches from his head.
Some idiot down range,
drunk or half-blind. What
my friend couldn't shake
for a long time:
the thud of that decision
burrowing into heartwood.

Abendlied

The sun slides away over the earth's rim.
The world faces its original pedigree—
night, and cold stars. The trees
that frame the dark with arching limbs

have relinquished their summer canopies
of sigh and whisper. Let the stars
tell stories—heroic disasters,
war, rape, mayhem. Cannibal histories

tacked up like connect-the-dots.
Trees bear nothing
but their own scaffolding. The streets
beneath them rustle with November.

Human day is done, loud and arrogant.
The world knows the peace of abandonment.

The Coal Smoke of Terre Haute

My mother used to say she couldn't hang out the laundry
because factory soot would settle like opinion.
Our alley was rough with cinders. People burned trash
in barrels. In the fall, old men burned leaves in the street.
Bars smelled of whiskey; churches smelled of Jesus.
Coal town, railroad town, union town.
Town of brakemen, shop men, bankers with soft hands
at the Rotary and Lions Club. The hominy mill,
American Can. Weeping women at Al-Anon,
shushed by the river the town turned its back on.
Town where our next-door neighbor, Uncle Bud,
a sad-eyed man in overalls, would take a BB gun
and shoot blue jays out of the trees.
Town where a man might be strapped to a gurney
and injected with pentobarbital
on the banks of the Wabash, far away.

December 8
thinking of William Stafford

It's neither a famous nor an infamous day.
It follows the line of other days
the way elephants enter a town, calmly holding
each other's tails. The way, if you are traveling
with a blind man, he puts his hand on your shoulder
out of practicality. Nobody gets lost. But
people do. Like those Japanese soldiers
on remote atolls: they were faithful to the cause
and to the stars, hearing only the drumbeat of surf.
People admired their fortitude—thirty years camping out.
But how did these soldiers feel when found?
The day after Pearl Harbor was bombed,
William Stafford didn't want to fight.
The government put him in a camp,
made him dig trenches, cut brush.
His supervisor wanted to shoot him.
The sound of wind in the trees was kind of like surf.
He felt a hand on his shoulder each day
after that.

Three Contemporaries

1. The Gentleman from Missouri

They remember him at the bus stop by St. Paul's.
His Bible, fluttering with post-it notes.
His tight suit. Was not known for being mates
with the faculty—no pub crawls, no sex jokes.
His mind an orrery in a high hall.
Prepped at Rockhurst, Stanford, Yale Law;
clerked for Roberts, fellowshipped with the Kochs.
Liked Pelagius, Yoram Hazony, Club for Growth.
Used the hometown courthouse as a photo-op.
Preacher of righteousness: liberty is not
freedom. It's walls, rules, norms, closets, clocks—
iron spheres soldered to their rods
circle the paradise of the post-liberal state.
Tick softly, and swing a big stick.

2. The Press Secretary

Politics means you find out who you are.
Serving a king is like living with an alcoholic.
So much apologizing to keep the faith,
so many bottles kicked under the bed,
so many hours theologizing his absence.
You have to obey in order to be loved.
You have to believe that he will sober up,
that lawlessness is the alternative
to the problem only he can solve.
The problem is you can't try hard enough—

to get good grades, make the team, earn the love
that will validate your faithfulness.
Then the problem changes: *others* must be punished
for not wanting to live in this paradise.

3. The Face of Justice

You can see the boy's face through the man's
midterm wrinkles, like you can look through a turbid creek
to still bottom, white sand and waving weeds.
The riffles of anger, privilege, just so much churn.
At Georgetown prep his small, surprising mouth
must have riled them a little:
cupidous purse, hint of motherly disapproval.
Some boys carry all their lives that drouth
to be varsity, to make it rain from mid-court.
It's pheromonal. The current under quiet homes,
quiet D.C. circles; school uniforms.
The upright lector in a hopsack blazer.
Buridan's ass, between sanctimony and license:
the love of God becomes the thirst for order.

God

The word becomes so important
it swells behind the eyes, presses the lids,
fills the mouth with phlegm. So important,
it creates the desire to live in a world of cartons,
staves, oil slicks, brass clocks, tics, a world
of sharpened knives and empty wastebaskets,
a world of subway tiles, gold teeth, nightlights,
nightingales, theses and antitheses,
microscopes, telescopes, sepsis and antisepsis,
a world of manners where servers greet us
with white gloves, where ghosts attack us,
where every desire is met with an equal and opposite
disaster. Where women wail, and men are silent,
until the opposite is true, and that ends it.

January

The great tiered entrance—where the President once spoke
doom to the Republic in a cashmere coat
that set off the pearl shimmer of his fantastical haircut,
then placed one hand on his unread childhood
Bible and swore to protect the constitution—
now swarms with a host in camo, Carhartt,
Timberland, Kevlar flack vests, surplus helmets,
Under Armour sweats—men in the orange caps of
    insurrection,
women, their faces inflamed with hope and rage,
hold up the pale screens of their phones,
imagining broadband angels, imagining they are not alone
but agents of history, the Spirit of the Age—
their Napoleon is not with them, he's safely home.
His white house hides him as the apple hides the worm.

Radical Chic

> *Traditional restraints and conventions broke down, one by one, until swords, clubs and rioting more or less replaced the ballot box.*
> —Mary Beard, *SPQR: A History of Ancient Rome*

Romans regretted the end of peaceful politics—
Gracchus the Tribune was killed with the leg of a chair,
his followers chased, slain, and dumped in the Tiber
for the affront of helping the poor.
                                        It's now chic
to carry a Glock on the floor of the House. Money
buys surrogates, costumes, selfies, the look
of mimed rebellion, shit-posting on Facebook
until farce turns tragedy. No longer funny,

the death of context, waving the starry ensign
of insurrection through the tear-gassed rotunda
under the painted stare of Charles Sumner
who was beaten in the Senate with a rebel's cane.

Meanwhile, Grant, who stopped the South at Shiloh,
gets his name chiseled off a school in San Francisco.

American Carnage

Invoking a violent dream against his father's
monstrous shaming, the president wrestles a ghost.
Panting, he struggles to dominate, to arrest
each flash grenade of thought. He'd rather
acquiesce to nothing than kowtow his stiff
coiffure to the sheet iron of the reality principle.
He is not a loser. He's not weak. He's the principal
effector of excellence, the gold standard, the best
Dauphin ever kept from a mother's breast,
totally valid, totally exonerated, the beautifully,
    savagely quiffed
wingman to Coronado in the wilderness.
Incited by his own vision of tawny eminence,
caressed by his own regard, he is at last
evicted. He nails his country to the mast.

Cocytus

January 13, 2021

O incongruous noon, white glare of snow,
a blue cast in the depths of every shadow.
Nine below, the world creaks, judders, smokes;
ice plates, ruts, sheets, ice teeth in the eaves
next door. The sun gauzy in a chemise of
fine particles. Sparrows shiver in bushes, puffed
all up to the size of dinner rolls. In back of
my garage, in the alley (a glacial river),
on the radio, in my idling car,
useless to affect the outcome, I hear the aged senator
slur the acquittal. "I shudder, and always will,"
Dante wrote, "remembering where
all gravity converged—that frozen pool—
yelping faces, made doglike by the chill."

Cups

America, you'll have to choose between Dutch rub and
 handshake,
between gang warfare and collective talk, between
Jesus on Parler, or Jesus in the eyes of your neighbor;
capillaries of rage, or enlarged pupils of recognition.
America, most of what you have done is a long con.
You've kept the cups in motion with the promise of
 revelation;
under one is a dream, under all the others, lack.
America, what is the point of this game?
The first one into the garden turns to lock the gate.
America, you need to live up to the dumb name
you got when you were badly drawn, and mostly made up.
America, don't make me fill in the blanks.

Compost Site

Mounds of shredded trees, leaves left
in sour drifts, the old house trailer
and the money box, the big Dutch grinder
with elaborate teeth. The sun is low;
long shadows creep out from the tool sheds.
I back the car up, empty the heavy sacks
of yellow parchment. Summer's broken texts
filed beside tree stumps, old sod,
grass clippings, rusted Christmas wreaths.
By the hurricane fence, the proprietor
has parked his Lincoln. The plates say
VIETNAM VET. Here's where his war
ends. Here's where wars never end—
where the little mouths of the world
take up our grievances.

Helicopter Sonnets

1. Training Flight

Winona, 2008

Pulse-beat out my window—the clear March air
shudders. Framed by the bare limbs
of the walnut tree, Apache helicopters hang
in attack formation. Fort McCoy, Wisconsin,
launched them—glittering, deliberate—
on maneuvers over the lulling farmland.
Nothing will burn beneath their rotors today
but that vibration hovered everywhere
above my childhood and my adolescence,
the insect hum, the quick drumbeat of death.
TV images of down-slashed rice grass,
water churned to froth by rotor-wash.
In the distance, little cartoon puffs
of ordnance smoke: the inscrutable war.

2. Qualifying Jump

MacDill Air Force Base, 1968

This is the year Sergeant Barry Sadler's
Green Beret Hymn blares from the radio.
All my friends sing it, wearing their plastic helmets
and toy M-1s. It's August now in Tampa;
my family's on vacation. We drive to the airfield
to watch my uncle, tense-necked Lieutenant-Colonel
in black boots, field pants, bulky chute,
stand in line with recruits half his age.
They climb in the cargo door. The chopper rocks
on its skids like a boxer on tiptoe.
The turbines rev, the ship begins to rise.
The downwash kicks up trash in the palmettos.
At twelve years old, I can feel the rotors' rush
through the chain link fence, a wind from Valhalla.

3. Surfari

Terre Haute, 1966

That summer I collected plastic Rat Finks
and listened to "Wipe Out" over and over
on the portable hi-fi in Gary's basement—
troll-laughter and the surge of drums
shook the speaker cloth. *My Three Sons*
were counseled on Channel Ten. In Cub Scout skits,
Maynard G. Krebs was our tutelary beatnik.
On the drugstore magazine rack, the latest issue
of *Sgt. Fury and His Howlin' Commandos*
was our guide to fighting the good war.
Meanwhile, on the evening news:
the grisly footage, the steadily mounting numbers.
The escalating drumbeat, the shriek of guitars,
the click of the tone arm's comforting retrieval.

4. Why We Are in Vietnam

Terre Haute, 1968

He's parked his Barracuda under the oaks
in Deming Park, by the municipal pool.
A blue geyser of chlorine
rises beneath the clatter of the high dive.
Framed in the uprights of a chain-link fence
three high school girls in floral-print bikinis
and sun tans, their hair glossily coiffed,
step from the shadow of the changing house.
He flicks his cigarette
into the roadside barrel, livid with wasps—
puts his hand to the ignition.
His engine awakens its brute staccato;
the girls turn, gracile and aroused.
Blue smoke stammers from his twin exhausts.

5. The Remains
Terre Haute, 1966

The white stone front of the interurban station,
the old distillery, the great grain elevator,
the river, with its burned-down bathing pavilion
where Theodore Dreiser watched girls in sodden woolens
rise from the muddy Wabash, as though from a baptism—
arranging their hair with a glamour they had read about in
Godey's Illustrated Monthly—and off Main Street,
the house where Eugene Debs, the famous socialist,
sat on his front porch and endured the scorn
of the Odd Fellows and Republicans—
I didn't see them. Or the stacked coffins
from Antietam, Verdun. Though any date
in the century you could have retrieved them,
down at the railroad station.

6. They'll Do It Every Time
Terre Haute, 1966

Twilight falls through the sheer curtains
in the parlor, and I am reading
the funny pages in the *Tribune Star*.
Major Hoople is there, and Moon Mullins,
with his bowler hat and cigars—they're in the parlor
reading the paper, blowing smoke wreaths.
In the kitchen, women large as oxen
are having thoughts, depicted as actual clouds
above their heads: visions of rolling pins
wielded as bludgeons. Their men see stars.
In *Alley Oop*, each man is caveman everyman
and citizen militant. He carries his cudgel
casually over his shoulder, like Teddy Roosevelt.
Whoever gets hit, he's sure deserves the credit.

7. Figures in a Landscape
Terre Haute, 1966

Twilight falls through the parlor curtains.
The TV is on, and Fess Parker
is wearing the skins of animals. He carries his rifle
casually over his shoulder, or in the crook
of his elbow, like an iron child.
Beside him, the ecumenical Mingo,
without his shirt, seems all eyebrows and scalp-lock;
his idea of friendship is adaptive capitulation.
In the background, the streaming electrons
assemble a wilderness—an ocean of trees—
that swallows all traces of anger or fear
in ashen pointillism. The original couple
moves toward the shadows, to disappear,
carrying weapons.

8. Apocalypse Now
France, 1979

Beaune, in cold Autumn rain
that falls on red-tiled roofs and sloping vineyards;
it soaks the hems of my jeans. I'm standing in
a crisply-tended park, reading a poster
for Coppola's new movie—an Asian sun
stains a crooked river; a squadron of Hueys
gathers like a plague of dragonflies.
Just then, the purr of a limousine. I turn
to see the Queen of England with her entourage
enroute to the medieval Hôtel Dieu.
I'm 22. I believe in the end of history
and rock-and-roll, the blandishments of my generation.
Later that night, on the Youth Hostel's television:
bearded youths. An Iranian revolution.

9. Redux
Winona, 2008

Tonight, I watch the opening scene
with students in my film class. At first, the screen
is plunged in darkness; then the rotors' pulse,
slowed and reverbed, cues the fade-in
to a strip of palms impossibly green. Vietnam
is as far away as D-Day, or Agincourt, but when
the chopper, flattened in a telephoto lens,
descends through ochre smoke, when they hear Morrison's
stoned break-up dirge, "This is the end, my friend,
of our elaborate plans," my students know it.
They know jarheads who blast *Ride of the Valkyries*
from growling Bradleys when they rush Fallujah.
Is it the end? The movie has no end.
When the credits roll, there's only the drumming of rain.

The Tower Variations

In the most photographed and videotaped day in the history of the world, the images of people jumping were the only images that became, by consensus, taboo—the only images from which Americans were proud to avert their eyes.
　—Tom Junod

*When tomorrow arrives we will love life
as it is, ordinarily shrewd
gray or colored,
no resurrection in it or end.*
　—Mahmoud Darwish

1.

In the photograph you tumble through empty space
against the backdrop of a building which is falling
more slowly and will be your sarcophagus.
You turn in the sun like any object.
The wind of your descent rattles your shirt
and tears at your pant cuffs;
your tie snaps like a failing chute.
I have dreamed it before; you must have dreamed it—
the stayless plummet, the wind in your throat—
only to wake in the darkness clutching your sheet.
Now there is no darkness, only the light
of a September morning, clear and pitiless,
and no one to wake you from your terrified shriek.

2.
Think of the morning before the day it became.
Your cup of coffee, a shy animal, trembled
as the subway passed underneath: the usual thunder,
friendly, efficient. Your split bagel seemed
a fragrant allegory of happiness.
The second hand walked round its post
on the wall clock, the cream cheese slept
in its small museum. The *Times*
offered its smudged headlines
and opinions. You shook your head
at the day's tragedies, skipping the obits.
Let's be clear about this:
had your name appeared among the missing,
you would have called in to demand a retraction.

3.
We didn't see you hit;
the cameras turned shyly away,
which means you're still falling
whenever we close our eyes. Falling still
in the darkened well of the psyche,
small speck downward against the blinding grid
of the towers. Without the end
of falling, it's as if we could stop time, as if
we might reach from a dream
and end your progress,
and let you live.
Often I think about your final minute:
the terrible compression, and speed, and knowledge,
life summing itself up as you came down upon it,
the landscape larger and larger until
you were part of it.

4.

In your apartment, people are quietly talking
as they gather up the important things.
Photographs in their frames sympathize, and are
　　poignant.
The phone rings, startling the cat.
By now everyone must know you are dead.
But who'll tell your shirts?
They sway slightly when the closet is opened,
arms down at their sides, soldiers at attention,
lightly starched. In single file
like a string of coming days.
Each collar swallows the hanger to its shank—
buttons gleam in the collar points,
like eyes that cannot close.

5.

On the front page of the paper,
the enormous wreckage—
twisted I-beams, cladding,
ganglia of steel.
In the foreground, Lilliputian
workmen in harness and yellow helmets:
explorers of the lost world.

6.

The President has sent the USS Theodore Roosevelt.
Aboard that ship, men and women ready themselves
to follow you into the dark with night-vision goggles
and M4 rifles. Tonight, in their bunks
under the shadowless fluorescents,
they are writing heartfelt banalities
on lined paper. Far beneath them,
the great propellors throb and churn the salt water.
So many lives in that honeycomb of steel
writing sentences that are irreversible,
set in motion by you, who wanted only
to sit with your coffee a moment and read the mail.

7.

> *... as many as 15 per cent of those innocent victims who died in the attacks were themselves Muslim men and women ...*
> —Asim Ashique

When the towers fell, there was rejoicing
in Nablus, in Jerusalem, in Hebron, Lebanon.
Those old, mythological places.
A few men handed out candies
and danced in the streets,
glad you were no kin of theirs,
you were a man falling in a story
carrying, as you fell past the world,
their pain and humiliation.
Should you hate or blame them?
You too walked the earth
with double vision—
a hell before you,
a paradise you imagined.
At the crowd's edge now
the bent figure approaches,
the black cloth of morning
pulled across her face.
Her hand is extended;
she's holding a ringing phone.
Who will take it,
the call from New York?
The voice from under the mountain.

8.
Thousands of telephones
buried under the rubble,
their buttons gone dark;
thousands of phone books
blown across the Hudson
like autumn leaves.
So many messages
haunting the catenary arc
of phone cables, lingering
under the guy wires
of microwave towers—
circling the earth like ghostly shadows,
a dark migration
that dims the satellites for a moment.
The unspoken sentences
of the rest of your life.

9.

Men at Ground Zero work all night
under floodlights, looking for you.
Having no body is so lonely.
From the beginning,
we dug doorways into the earth,
folded the loved body in a posture of sleep,
added what we thought it would need:
a pair of shoes, a pouch of corn,
flowers, an obsidian knife.
We wet these with our tears,
then piled earth over them. Our
sorrow is a door that keeps opening.
An endless limit.
Our hands lift in supplication
at the lip of the world;
we find its taste both bitter and sweet.
The lid that closes tight, keeps its perfume.

10.

My daughter draws flags with uneven crayon stripes
and, in the left-handed corner, a jumble of angry stars.
She stands in the back yard and sings *America the Beautiful*
at the top of her lungs. I want to tell her to be more ironic;
what you want is simple: not to be dead.
Her country is where she lives—sunflowers by the fence,
the porch, the swing set. It's a lump in her throat,
like a low-grade fever. And flags are everywhere—
in store windows, on car aerials, bumpers, tailgates,
jacket lapels. A manic multiplication.
Never mind that you would have preferred
the flag of the country called "everyday,"
whose standard is the tea towel with crossed spoons.
Or the nation called "satisfying labor,"
whose coat of arms is the entrance to the subway.

11.
Early frost killed the basil
and the last of summer's tomatoes.
The leaves on the walnut,
weighted with silver,
fell with a wet patter.
The lake was white with mist
and a single heron
stood hunched in his cloak
like a brooding ambassador.
Sunlight struck the earth
with an iron ring.
On the kitchen radio
the U.N. relief worker said,
"I stood down
by the yellow tape, and the smell
of hot plastic and rotting flesh
took me back to the early '80s,
to the Peshawar valley
after the Red Army
had pounded a village.
The women all had the same look,
searching the rubble
for pieces of someone they loved."

12.

An image from CNN:
the Afghan desert,
the small figure of a man
in caftan and turban,
surrounded by white packages,
their banners fluttering
with indecipherable signs.
He does not know if
they carry food or bombs.
Their number extends to his horizon—
good or bad intentions
kicked out of the rear door of an airplane
at an altitude too great
to tell the difference.

13.
After launch, the wings unfold for lift,
the airscoop is exposed, and the turbofan engine
is switched on for cruise flight. Over water, the missile
uses inertial guidance or GPS.
Once over land, the Tomahawk's path is aided
by Terrain Contour Matching Terminal guidance, which
is provided by Digital Scene Matching Area Correlation,
and is accurate to ten meters. It's the targets that can't be relied on
to be military. To not be women and children.
"The savages make war upon us without respect to age or sex,"
said Thos. Jefferson, detailing the King's malfeasance.
After which, colonists burned the Ohio towns
of the Cherokee and the Seneca.
One war chief said, "Their intention is to exterminate us."
War whoop. Ambush by night. Ash handle and totem feather.
Slash of a jet trail over the Indian Ocean.

14.
Past my kitchen window now,
every two minutes,
the yellow flicker of a walnut leaf
twirls as it plummets—a small
spinnaker of descent.
The place it falls from reveals a little more
autumn sky—
in the end, there is only
the temple of blue
and the veins of hard shadow
and the burial mound of leaves.

15.

The Office of Homeland Security

The asters are secure in their radiant faces.
The walnut leaves are secure in their vagrant piles.
The crows are secure in their ragged squadrons.
The moon is secure in the arms of the white pine.

16.
I wish you were here to see my daughters dance
to the Goldberg variations.
They make such lumbering graceful gestures
in their dress-up tutus. When they jump
the record skips—our turntable seems as antiquated
as the clavichord Goldberg played
(according to the liner notes)
to help a Russian ambassador sleep.
Outside, the dusk is violet;
a string of colored Christmas lights
decorates the house across the street.
You are somewhere under a Himalaya of concrete,
and aluminum flashing, and asbestos insulation
crushed to eerie ash—all lying under
hard autumn stars that once,
like your days, seemed bright and endless
and now are all named and ancient.

The thought of which can make it hard to sleep.

17.
As darkness falls, it's mirrored in the window
like a star map, or night traffic. From the branches
dangle an odd assortment of ornaments
collected in our family's life:
a Swedish mitten, a Pooh bear, a knitted bird,
a mirrored ball, a reindeer made of Popsicle sticks
with glued-on eyes, a blown-glass angel,
a candy cane still in its crinkled wrapper.
Things giddy and random,
as if tossed by a whirlwind
then frozen mid-descent,
caught in the arms of this tree—
living and fragrant, and commemorative.

18.

Yesterday New York's mayor claimed the fires were out
under the debris-mountain, the parking garage of fragments.
Meanwhile, the men who lit them hid in caves
issuing proclamations in scratchy videos.
Didn't we begin in caves? Tracing images with our fingers,
in ochre, and charcoal, and animal tallow,
watching what we depicted become more beautiful
than experience, so we might surmount death, so we might affirm
what comes in at the eye belongs in the soul
to kindle desire, and deepen the logic of dreams.
Even now, telling the story, writing this poem
to you, I hold up the world you were part of,
giving shape to the paradise that torments me.

19.

> ... *the World Trade Center should become a representation of man's ability to find greatness.*
>   —Minoru Yamasaki, World Trade Center architect

At sunset they were rich with the sun's gilding;
at night, they rose like converging ladders of light
and people loved them. "I feel this way about it,"
said the architect, "World trade means world peace."
His optimism climbed thirteen hundred feet.
But most of the time they stood dull as children's blocks,
two anodized Tylenol, white grocery lists,
twin exclamation marks at the end of a century
of excess. "Filing cabinets," Mumford called them.
Two candle pins at Broadway's lower reach.
Yet on the day they were hit, they burned like torches.
When they went down, they went down like ships,
leaving in their absence sudden vistas
through which we glimpsed—not peace—but its opposite.

20.

The poster on the wall, a crummy Xerox,
holds the features of someone who's missing.
The weather has faded it; the details are bleaching
into the paper. The simple message
soon will be illegible, along with the number
we could call to report, should the unlikely happen,
should someone pass us in the street who was standing
on the eightieth floor, waiting to go to a meeting,
before the roar of angels and the flame.

Fall Palette

Out Of Eden

The high gate clanged
and trash blew against the fence.
We could see the angels in their dormitories,
the lighted doorway of the chapel
we'd never enter again.
The river flowed under the gate
and into the darkness, and we followed it.
After the first bend, we didn't look back.
The land unfolded
its lengthening question.
In new forests, wolves
chased deer. Hawks circled.
Frogs called in the marshes.

Shall I not extend my hand
to you, stranger,
when we meet
in this wilderness?

Rapturous Decay

after a fabric installation by Liz Miller

Parade of little prominences
so papery, so *sec*; the crisp
can almost walk
in sufficient wind.
Are they falling or rising?
Is that a bridge or a doorway?
Whose spire is draped? Whose
wings are shrouded over whose
filigreed gills? The details
are in the devil. Once
you kicked your way through a
barricade of such dry fragrances
and gestures—a drift
of skins cast off
by an indifferent season.
Underneath, the same
earth, with a new hat,
the same death and its promises.

2.
If you cut out enough,
what's left is lace, its
absence repeated along the fold.
What ends is continuing
on the reverse edge.
"Cut it out," she said,
as if we could.

3.
Did we notice the bird is a frond?
Or that its wing was leveraged
in the breast of something
that sought the sun?

4.
The end was burning all along—
green, then gold.
As if value could be added by asphyxiation.
How many fancy masks were left behind
by the wind, then impressed by the rain?
How many gestures froze in their noble wrappers?
All of you who come after
follow the fish-line of intention.
The maker is gone but
not her independence.

Michigan Sonnet

Sumac bleeds against high tension towers.
There's misery in the second growth, the grey
skies like gauze; it's November
in the Consumer's Power right-of-way.

Tickseeds scatter like caltrops. Fringed eyelids
of former lace-queens, wands of mullein. Scrub oak
leaves don't vanish the way maple leaves did
(on fire), they cling and shudder as the first bleak

hard pellets gather in the cracks
of the sidewalk in front of your ranch house.
It's Saturday morning; you're kicking back

eating Fruit Loops and watching *Space Ghost*
on Channel 50—the antenna's bad—
and snow is filling the cartoon universe.

Contemplating A Phrase from Lewis Mumford

Downtown on a grey afternoon, walking
midwestern Main Street business blocks
past decayed storefronts whose redbrick cornices
and Roman windows date from the Age of Garfield—
sawdust, armbands, spittoons, the reek
of the outhouse, the brewery's yeast-perfume,
chickens in backyards, rhubarb and morning glory,
whores above the millinery shop on Third Street,
dentists and opium, William Morris wallpaper,
medals for Antietam and Sunday school,
the clop-clop of carriage horses under
umbrageous tunnels of elm—gone,
"those collective energies confronted and risen to."
Parking lot, parking lot, gas station, parking lot.

Simmer

A burner on "medium high" is made to simmer
the pot in which the barnyard bird you dragged
from the chopping block (blood like a red flag)
floats, plucked and eviscerated. The knife glimmered
when it sectioned the carrots. So much for rain
glazing the wheelbarrow. The stark poles
of experience, if you took a poll,
would show all the horses who have felt the rein
across their necks—or each woodpecker worrying the suet
in its cage, or the prophet in his sandals
nailed to a wall—would say the black jug has two handles
because there is more than one way to do it
justice. The jug may pass
from hand to hand, but it comes to you at last.

The Anthropocene

Birthday parties, love affairs, civilizations,
cigarettes, documentaries,

bicycles, dogs, wallpaper, children,
waterfalls, acorns, paper clips,

clouds, ships, gods,
all have their end. After a million

more or less ambitious, busy springs,
filling the strata with bones and footprints,

building the resume, building credit, depositing night soil,
all evidence of our diligence, our faith in kismet, uplift,

vanishes, along with the conversation.
You can sit at a table at an outdoor restaurant

all afternoon and we'll never turn up. Though
the affair continues, after a fashion,

in the molecule, the particle, the gene,
the sparkle of sun on a fragment,

the rustle of a plastic bag in a dry riverbed.

Say Yes to Michigan

Say it. Please. I
absolve you if you are lying.
You don't feel enthusiastic?
You don't want to be false?
Even I sometimes feel that way—less than
sanguine, wanting less, growing weary of
too much scenery, pines and lakes that
overwhelm, a surfeit of jet-skis, too
many winking, perfect cherries.
I sometimes want to be alone,
crossing the urban street and
having a thought that is not recreational
in the least—brooding, or feeling a
gust of grief, that's ok. But arrowed
(as you must be) toward the next
near minute, kept by default from
no, isn't it easier to say yes? To embrace the
obvious, which can't be your fault,
which can't be voided or fought?

Normal School

1913, Winona, Minnesota

In your rustling dress,
you have attended the organizational meeting
of the Schubert Society
and a lecture on deportment.
Your stockings are woolen,
your manners quasi-Victorian,
learned at church suppers
and ice cream socials.
Last year, you and your sister
braided each other's hair
and stayed up half the night
reading *Little Women*
by smuggled candlelight.
Jo was your Book of Revelation.
Now, on the porch of your residence hall
some fellow with a mandolin
is singing the Whiffenpoof song
while you lean on the casement,
thinking of Mama boiling cabbage,
washing the cut-glass pickle dish,
beating the parlor rug
with an iron rod.

In the laboratory school
across the street: plaster busts
of Roman emperors,
photographs of the Parthenon,
beakers, microscopes,
a gymnasium,

something called "basket-ball."
Every weekday the children come
to your classroom, boys in knee-pants,
the girls in satin bows, and
your professor observes you,
holding his watch
as you practice sums,
draw sentence diagrams,
read aloud from Tennyson.

Far out on the prairie,
past Sleepy Eye and Slayton,
is a clapboard schoolhouse—
it's empty,
except for the tick
of the Regulator clock.
The floor is swept underneath the pot-bellied stove.
The slates are washed and stacked.

Across the harvested fields,
Under cold farmhouse gables
in iron beds, under threadbare quilts,
children toss in their sleep;
they are waiting for you,
tall ambassador,
with your high-button shoes
and your boxes of
white, white chalk.

Polonius

The weather today calls for a wintry mix.
Your symptoms might range from moderate to severe.
Results may vary. Always consult your physician.
Offer not valid in the following states:
satisfaction, Whirlpool, nourishment, despair.
If the flame sputters, adjust the fuel-to-air ratio.
If the light is on, consult your service manual.
GREETINGS! This product may contain soy or peanuts.
Please turn the power off before attempting repair.
For best results, use before October 12.
Results are based upon a clinical test.
If the garment does not fit you, or does not suit you,
please return it to the above address.

Remember to include
a valid proof of purchase.

Landscape

from "Paysage" by Robert Desnos

I once dreamed of love. I still do, but love
is no longer this bouquet of lilies and roses
perfuming the adjacent wilderness
where a flame burned at the end of the bridle path.

I once dreamed of loving. I still do, but love
is no longer the lightning which discharged
its heat on battlements; illuminated, discomposed
in a lurid flash, our farewell at the crossroads.

Love is the flint-spark under my shoes in the night,
it's the word no dictionary in the world can translate,
that foam on the sea, and in the sky, that cloud …

to grow old is to become rigid and luminous—
boulevards without names, cords without knots.
I can feel myself hardening with the landscape.

Against The Gnostics

We water the garden in the dusk.
The sprinkler's fantail, a shimmer of beads,
arches over the orbs of the tomatoes
and the basil's dense umbrellas,
the sulfurous fluttery tubas of the squash blossoms,
until the earth turns moist and then exhales
its mouthwash of fungus and chocolate,
the fervid tang of worms.
At the end of fifteen minutes, the spigot squeaks.
For a long time after,
there is only the sound of water
dripping from the Presbyterian leaves;
a robin runs the rows in his saffron leggings,
probing for dinner, soiling his breast with the world.

Requiem

I get up and put on my war pajamas
and go downstairs; the coffee is black as war.
The oatmeal is warm as a small local war.
In the paper they are advertising a war sale;
the clothes of war are half off.
There are coupons you can cut along the dotted line
for canned war, for frozen war.
I brush my teeth with the paste of war
and shower in a barrage of war water.
I drive to work, the fumes of heroic sacrifice
rising from my exhaust pipe.
All day long I am doing war work.
At night I relax with a shot of war on ice.
In my dreams, the war is never over.

Pulling Out

August 19, 2010

That was the summer the war ended
(the other war, and it wasn't exactly over).
Some of them would be staying,
but most were going
home, soldiers in digi-camo battle dress
like abstract expressionist
curtains from the 50s, or jigsaw puzzles.
You could see they'd been put together,
strapped down in jump seats in the fuselage
of a C130, or buckled in the leviathan bed
of an armored Stryker. They moved
down highways that started nowhere
and ended nowhere, the desert horizon
like a razor cut on the infinite.

Remember the hand-lettered signs
that hung in our neighborhood, crying
"No Blood For Oil"? (that was
2002—the year of the "smoking gun"
when a bedsheet hung over La Guernica).
But oil is blood, "blood of the earth,
the blood of victory" they said
in 1918, when they ended
the War to End all Wars
and set up the next one.
Just ask the Romanians, whose oilfields
were Hitler's Christmas cracker. The growling
Panzer divisions and whistling Stukas needed
the blood of the earth

to shed the blood of men.
Ask the Iraqi divisions who stood with
their hands on their heads
in front of American tanks,
in that other Gulf war,
for that other President
Bush.
    So this was the end
of summer; like every summer
we came home from vacation and dried out our tent,
flipped through the mail, weeded the garden,
read the newspaper. IT'S OVER, the headline said:
the last Stryker division crossed the frontier.
And on the next page, the dry account
from Superior: a Wisconsin vet
shot his wife, his daughter, his pets
and then put the still-hot pistol into his mouth.

Fall Palette

The lobes of the oak leaves
are sometimes pale violet
like evening above
the Avenida da Liberdade
in Lisbon; are sometimes
the shellacked brown
saddle leather of chestnuts
in paper sacks sold
by Moroccan immigrants
beside their smoking braziers.
Birch leaves are so many kinds of yellow—
mustard to lemon, wan
almost-tan, the hue of brittle clipped
obituaries in the back of a prayer book,
or yellowed high school sports statistics
we found when we cleaned out the old desk.
Crimson lipstick stains
the teeth of that sumac, but
the maple's radial star
is the blare of a French horn,
the muzzle-flash of a shotgun. Yet
the little leaves of the understory—
thin wildflowers, ferns—

are still green, the pale
green of an early spring
raincoat worn by Audrey Hepburn
who lies down in the deep moss
looking up at the trees.
She is solemn, and low.
It's been fun, but
she might have to move to New York.
Summer has
definitely gone.

Notes

"Fair Haired Lads Pass," "Loch Ness," "Slighe," and "The Fall of Foyers" refer to places on the Great Glen Way, a hiking path in central Scotland that follows both sides of Loch Ness.

"Comus" refers to a Greek god of "festivity, revels and nocturnal dalliances," as Wikipedia puts it.

"Sonnenizio Based on a Line from Terrance Hayes" refers to a poetic form invented by Kim Addonizio. A sonnenizio requires the poet to take a line from another poet's work and use it as the first line of a new 14-line poem; every subsequent line in the poem must use a word from the borrowed line. The line I employ is from Hayes' *American Sonnets for My Past and Future Assassin*, a book that helped get me through the last years of the Trump administration.

"The Coal Smoke of Terre Haute" makes oblique reference to the United States Penitentiary outside of the city, which houses a federal execution chamber.

"Three Contemporaries" refers to Josh Hawley, Kayley McEnany, and Brett Kavanaugh.

"Cocytus" refers to the frozen lake at the lowest level of Dante's *Inferno*, reserved for frauds and traitors.

In the Helicopter Sonnets, "Why We Are in Vietnam" refers to a famous speech given by President Johnson justifying his escalation of America's involvement in the war. "They'll Do It Every Time" refers to a number of newspaper comics: Jimmy Hatlo's *They'll Do It Every Time*, Gene Ahern's

Our Boarding House (starring Major Hoople), and Frank Willards' *Moon Mullins*. All three comics originated in the 1920s and preserved, as in amber, the ethos of pre-war, working-class America. *Alley Oop* was also a popular newspaper comic strip; its titular hero was a caveman living in the land of Moo. "Figures in a Landscape" refers to the television show *Daniel Boone*, which ran from 1964 to 1970.

"Say Yes to Michigan" was a nearly ubiquitous advertising slogan for the state's tourist industry in the 1980s.

Acknowledgements

My gratitude to the journals, websites, and anthologies in which a number of these poems previously appeared: *Split Rock Review; Poetry East; Twyckenham Notes; TriQuarterly; Ocooch Mountain Echo; Terrain.org; The Friends of William Stafford Journal & Newsletter; Waters Deep: A Great Lake Poetry Anthology; Undocumented: Great Lakes Poets Laureate on Social Justice; Poetry in Michigan/Michigan in Poetry.*

"Out of Eden" was written for the cantata of the same name composed by David Kassler.

"Fall Palette" first appeared as a broadside by Zachariah Selley.

"The Office of Homeland Security" first appeared as a broadside by Sutton Hoo Press.

My immense gratitude to Richard Jones, whose steadfast editorial support over the years has meant so much. Thanks to Reg Gibbons for wise mentorship. Thanks to my poetry group in Winona, especially Orv Lund, Ken McCullough, and Scott Lowery, whose many suggestions helped shape these poems. Thanks to Steven Hind and Albert Goldbarth for their enthusiastic reception of these poems. Thanks to Kim Chapman for a lifetime of conversation. Thanks to Emilio DeGrazia, who advocated for this book. Thanks to Tom Driscoll, the captain of Shipwreckt Books, for taking a genial and collaborative approach to publishing.

Thanks to my colleagues at the Winona State University English Department for more than two decades of literary conversation. Thanks to my poetry students who have kept me curious and humble over the years.

Thanks to my children for their encouragement and affection and for allowing me to grow up with them.

Thanks to my sister, who knew what good poetry was before I did, and whose courage and resilience continue to inspire me.

Thanks to my partner and best reader, Laura Armstrong, who gave this manuscript the same deep attention she gives to all aspects of our life together.

About the Poet

James Armstrong taught English and Creative Writing at Winona State University in Winona, Minnesota, for 24 years. He was Winona's first Poet Laureate. He helps run the Maria W. Faust Sonnet Contest and plays guitar in the Bell House Band.

Printed in the USA
CPSIA information can be obtained
at www.ICGtesting.com
LVHW090507180724
785774LV00002B/248